including
- *Life and Background*
- *List of Characters*
- Our Town *Genealogy*
- *Brief Plot Synopsis*
- *Summaries & Critical Commentaries*
- *Character Analyses*
- *Critical Essays*
    Thematic Structure
    Structure and Technique
    Language and Style
    Wilder's Philosophy
    Our Town from the Current Perspective
- *Suggested Essay Questions*
- *Selected Bibliography*

by
Mary Ellen Snodgrass, M.A.
Former Chair, Dept. of English
Hickory High School
Hickory, North Carolina

NEW EDITION

Cliffs Notes
INCORPORATED
LINCOLN, NEBRASKA 68501

Editor

Gary Carey, M.A.
University of Colorado

Consulting Editor

James L. Roberts, Ph.D.
Department of English
University of Nebraska

ISBN 0-8220-0967-6
© Copyright 1990
by
Cliffs Notes, Inc.
All Rights Reserved
Printed in U.S.A.

1999 Printing

The Cliffs Notes logo, the names "Cliffs" and "Cliffs Notes," and the black and yellow diagonal-stripe cover design are all registered trademarks belonging to Cliffs Notes, Inc., and may not be used in whole or in part without written permission.

Cliffs Notes, Inc.   Lincoln, Nebraska

CONTENTS

Life and Background 5

List of Characters 7

Our Town Genealogy 10

Brief Plot Synopsis 11

Summaries & Critical Commentaries
    Act I 13
    Act II 20
    Act III 27

Character Analyses
    Emily Webb Gibbs 34
    George Gibbs 35
    Editor Charles Webb 37
    Doctor Frank Gibbs 37
    Mrs. Julia Gibbs and Mrs. Myrtle Webb 38
    The Stage Manager 39

Critical Essays
    Thematic Structure 40
    Structure and Technique 41
    Language and Style 43
    Wilder's Philosophy 44
    Our Town from the Current Perspective 44

Suggested Essay Questions 46

Related Research Projects 47

Selected Bibliography 48

OUR TOWN
Notes

LIFE AND BACKGROUND

Thornton Niven Wilder's *Our Town* is a major work in the canon of American theater. Translated and produced throughout the world, it has been called a poetic chronicle of life and death. First produced at the McCarter Theatre in Princeton, New Jersey, on January 22, 1938, the play wavered in Boston, was moved to New York, and, to the surprise of both the playwright and his collaborators, won a Pulitzer Prize as the best play of the season. *Our Town* remains a perennial favorite among directors, particularly in small-town productions.

Our Town pays tribute to traditional American hometown values. Deceptively simple in structure and tone, the play represents many of the author's humanistic views. In an age obsessed with the unusual and the bizarre, the neurotic and the psychotic, Wilder turns his attention to the attributes and universality of the ordinary citizen. Making no apologies for his nostalgic journey into the past, he asserts his optimism in an age of pessimism.

Although Wilder was born in Madison, Wisconsin, April 17, 1897, his tastes are not regional. He tends toward the mainstream of the American tradition. Both of Wilder's grandfathers were clergymen, and he himself considered going into the ministry. His parents — Amos Parker Wilder and Isabella Thornton Wilder — believed strongly in culture and stressed religion, education, and intellectual pursuits to their five children.

Early in his son's life, Amos Wilder studied economics and edited the *Wisconsin State Journal*. Through his friend President Taft, he was named America's Consulate-General to Hong Kong in 1906. Thornton Wilder, therefore, received his early education in Chinese missionary schools in Hong Kong, Chefoo, and Shanghai. Upon completing high school in Berkeley, California, in 1915, he attended Oberlin

College for two years, served in the coast artillery in 1918, and graduated from Yale in 1920 with a degree in classical literature.

From 1920 to 1921, Wilder spent a year studying archeology at the American Academy in Rome, where he participated in the excavation of an Etruscan roadway. He returned to America to teach French and to counsel at a prep school in Lawrenceville, New Jersey; he completed a master's degree in English from Princeton in 1926. Seven years later, Wilder was able to live on the income of his writing.

In 1930, however, Wilder returned to the classroom, teaching drama and poetry at the University of Chicago, a position he retained until 1936. In this same period, he worked for several motion picture studios as a screenwriter. During World War II, he served as an air intelligence officer and achieved the rank of lieutenant colonel. For his wartime contributions, he earned the Legion of Merit, Bronze Star, Legion d'Honneur, and honorary membership in the Order of the British Empire.

From 1950 to 1951, he gave the Charles Eliot Norton Lectures in poetry at Harvard. By the spring of 1962, Wilder, flagging somewhat in health, retired to Douglas, a small town in the Arizona desert, where he allowed himself the luxury of a two-year respite. Among the locals, Thornton was known as "Doc." Until his death in Hamden, Connecticut, in 1975, Wilder lived with his sister, novelist Isabel Wilder, and spent his time writing and traveling.

Wilder's acclaim is based mainly upon his novels, particularly *The Bridge of San Luis Rey* (1927), which won a Pulitzer Prize and established his popularity after being adapted for film and television, and *The Ides of March* (1948). His most famous plays are *Our Town* (1938), which was filmed in 1940 and reproduced as a TV musical in 1955; *The Skin of Our Teeth* (1942), a Pulitzer Prize-winning historical drama about Julius Caesar; and *The Matchmaker* (1954), which forms the basis for the Broadway musical and Hollywood movie *Hello, Dolly* (1963). As a result of his success, in 1965 Wilder became the first recipient of the National Medal for Literature.

The appeal of most of Wilder's plays is based on classic human values, which he draws from myth, fable, and parable as well as from the influence of James Joyce, André Gide, Marcel Proust, T. S. Eliot, Ezra Pound, Anatole France, and Gertrude Stein. Although it is not immediately apparent in *Our Town*, the play is grounded on a humanism which depicts life as both terrifying and wonderful. The author emphasizes the spark of immortality that exists in each human spirit.

MAJOR WORKS

The Cabala, novel, 1926.
The Bridge of San Luis Rey, novel, 1927.
The Angel That Troubled the Waters, and Other Plays, drama, 1928.
The Woman of Andros, novel, 1930.
The Long Christmas Dinner, and Other Plays in One Act, drama, 1931.
Lucrece, drama, 1933.
Heaven's My Destination, novel, 1935.
Our Town, drama, 1938.
The Merchant of Yonkers, drama, 1938.
Our Town, screenplay, 1940.
The Skin of Our Teeth, historical drama, 1942.
Shadow of a Doubt, screenplay, 1942.
Our Century, drama, 1947.
The Ides of March, novel, 1948.
The Matchmaker, drama, 1954.
The Alcestiad, drama, 1955.
The Matchmaker, screenplay, 1958.
The Seven Deadly Sins, drama cycle, 1964.
The Seven Ages of Man, drama cycle, 1964.
The Eighth Day, novel, 1967.
Theophilus North, novel, 1973.

LIST OF CHARACTERS

Stage Manager

The narrator, who also plays the roles of master of ceremonies, Mrs. Forrest, Mr. Morgan, and a minister. He guides Emily in her return to the living world.

Dr. Frank Gibbs

The town's doctor, who is returning from delivering the Goruslawski twins during the first act. He is the father of George and Rebecca Gibbs.

Mrs. Julia Hersey Gibbs

Dr. Gibbs' wife, who represents a typical housewife in the first two acts; in the final act, she is seen as a spirit.

George Gibbs

Dr. and Mrs. Gibbs' sixteen-year-old son, who discovers his love for Emily, marries her in the second act, and grieves for her loss in the third act.

Rebecca Gibbs

Dr. and Mrs. Gibbs' daughter, who is four years younger than George. She realizes that Grover's Corners is part of New Hampshire, part of America, part of the world, the universe. This expanding image is central to Wilder's theme.

Mr. Charles Webb

The editor and publisher of the *Sentinel,* the town's newspaper, and one of its most important citizens. He lives across from the Gibbs family.

Mrs. Myrtle Webb

Charles Webb's wife, who reveals her character through her conversation with Mrs. Gibbs; she represents the typical mother and housewife.

Emily Webb Gibbs

The Webbs' intelligent daughter, who grows up during the play, joins the two major families when she marries George Gibbs, and dies later during childbirth.

Wallace "Wally" Webb

Emily's younger brother and one of the spirits in the last act. In Act III, we discover that he died suddenly from a ruptured appendix while on a Boy Scout trip.

Simon Stimson

The organist of the Congregational Church who is the subject of town gossip because of his alcoholism. As a suicide who hangs himself in the attic, Simon's memories of the past are negative.

Mrs. Louella Soames

A local busybody who clucks over Simon's alcoholism and idealizes George and Emily's marriage. She is a spirit in the last act.

Howie Newsome

The milkman who guides a seventeen-year-old horse named Bessie. Howie appears during Emily's return to the past in the last act.

Joe Crowell, Jr.

Joe is the paper boy in the first act and also during the flashback, when Emily returns to life. A scholar at Massachusetts Tech, he is killed in France during World War I before he can use his education.

Si Crowell

Joe's younger brother, who takes Joe's job as paper boy in Act II to indicate the passage of time.

Samuel "Sam" Craig

The son of Julia Gibbs' sister Carey, he comes back from Buffalo after twelve years' absence. He provides exposition in the last act.

Joe Stoddard

The town undertaker, who provides background information in the third act.

Constable Bill Warren

The town law enforcement officer, whose duties require him to be sure that doors are locked and that drain pipes are adequate. On February 7, 1899, he saves a man from freezing to death.

Our Town Genealogy

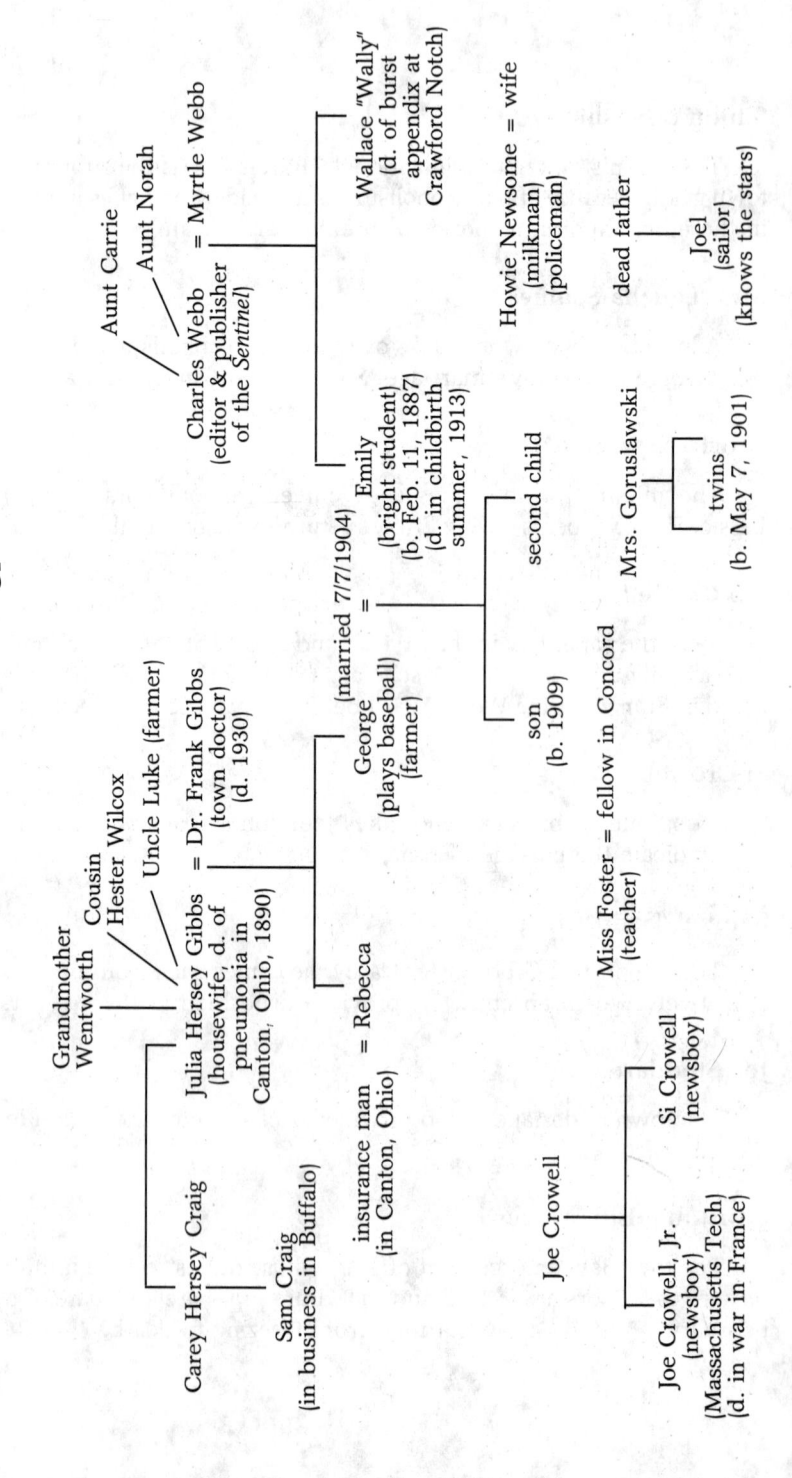

- Grandmother Wentworth
  - Carey Hersey Craig
    - Sam Craig (in business in Buffalo)
  - Julia Hersey Gibbs (housewife, d. of pneumonia in Canton, Ohio, 1890) = Dr. Frank Gibbs (town doctor) (d. 1930)
    - Rebecca = insurance man (in Canton, Ohio)
    - George (plays baseball) (farmer) — (married 7/7/1904) = Emily (bright student) (b. Feb. 11, 1887) (d. in childbirth summer, 1913)
      - son (b. 1909)
      - second child
- Cousin Hester Wilcox
- Uncle Luke (farmer)

- Aunt Carrie
- Aunt Norah
- Charles Webb (editor & publisher of the *Sentinel*) = Myrtle Webb
  - Wallace "Wally" (d. of burst appendix at Crawford Notch)
  - Emily (see above)

Howie Newsome = wife (milkman) (policeman)

dead father
- Joel (sailor) (knows the stars)

Miss Foster = fellow in Concord (teacher)

Mrs. Goruslawski
- twins (b. May 7, 1901)

Joe Crowell
- Joe Crowell, Jr. (newsboy) (Massachusetts Tech) (d. in war in France)
- Si Crowell (newsboy)

Professor Willard

A faculty member of State University who recites facts about Grover's Corners.

BRIEF PLOT SYNOPSIS

Act I, which Wilder calls "Daily Life," is a re-creation of the normal daily activities found in a small New Hampshire town. The act opens with the appearance of the Stage Manager, who speaks directly to the audience. He tells where all of the main buildings of the town are located and gives pertinent facts about Grover's Corners. Then he introduces us to the Webbs and the Gibbses, who are two of the town's main families.

After the introduction by the Stage Manager, the milkman and paper boy arrive and signal the official opening of the action of the play. Then the representative families begin to assemble for breakfast. First, the mother in each family tries to get her children up, dressed, fed, and off to school. After the children leave, the two mothers (Mrs. Webb and Mrs. Gibbs) meet for a chat. The Stage Manager returns and states more facts about the town. By this time, the day has passed by. Emily Webb and George Gibbs come home from school. George is struggling with schoolwork; Emily is the best student in her class. The two young people arrange a way so that Emily can assist George.

The Stage Manager returns and tells more about the town. Mrs. Webb and Mrs. Gibbs attend weekly choir rehearsal. Afterward, they discuss the organist's drinking. That night, Mrs. Gibbs tells her husband that the organist's drinking problem is the worst she has ever seen. The constable strolls by on patrol. This passage signals the end of a typical day.

The second act occurs some years later. After more comments by the Stage Manager, Mrs. Gibbs and Mrs. Webb return to the stage to prepare for a wedding. Both receive deliveries from the milkman and invite him and his wife to the ceremony.

George Gibbs comes downstairs and tells his mother that he is going across the yard to see Emily, his girl; they are to be married later that day. When he reaches the Webbs' house, Mrs. Webb reminds him that the groom should not see the bride on the day of the wedding. George talks to his future father-in-law until Mrs. Webb reappears and sends George home so that Emily can come downstairs to breakfast.

The Stage Manager then **turns back time** to the day when George and Emily first discover their love for each other. George stops Emily on their way home from school. He has just been elected president of the senior class; Emily is secretary-treasurer. He asks her why she is mad at him. Emily admonishes George for immersing himself in baseball and forgetting his friends. He assures Emily that he has not forgotten her. George emphasizes that Emily is special to him and that she remains in his thoughts. Emily feels that she is mistaken about George and returns his affection. They part after having acknowledged their mutual love.

The Stage Manager enters and explains that he will serve as minister and makes further comments about weddings. Mrs. Webb expresses fear about losing her daughter. Then George owns up to momentary doubts about getting married. In the meantime, Emily relates her qualms to her father. As soon as George and Emily see each other, they overcome their fears.

The ceremony takes place in the background while the audience hears the comments of Mrs. Soames, a wedding guest. Then the Stage Manager returns in his original persona to make closing remarks.

The third act occurs in the cemetery at the burial of Emily Webb Gibbs, who has just died in childbirth and left her husband and four-year-old son. Like any newcomer, she is uneasy among the dead; she wonders how long the feeling will last. After the mourners leave the cemetery, she longs to return to life for a single day. The other spirits try to dissuade her, but she insists.

Emily chooses to relive her twelfth birthday, but when she returns to earth, she discovers that people live their lives without appreciating or sharing the moment of living. They overlook the joy found in simple everyday activities. Emotionally unable to endure a full day of her past, Emily returns to the cemetery. There, at night, she watches George come to grieve at her grave. Emily perceives that the living understand little about death and even less about being alive.

SUMMARIES & CRITICAL COMMENTARIES

ACT I

Summary

Act I begins with no curtain; the Stage Manager simply appears onstage and brings in two tables, some chairs, and a bench. As the house lights dim, he speaks directly to the audience, telling them who wrote and directed the play, as well as necessary facts about Grover's Corners, New Hampshire, "just across the Massachusetts line." He announces the time as being just before dawn on May 7, 1901. He delineates the layout of the town, pointing out six churches, the railroad tracks, the town hall and jail, the post office, and Polish Town, where the minority families live. He is able to look into the future and announce when the first automobile will reach town.

The Stage Manager points to an imaginary spot downstage and explains that Doc Gibbs lives in this house. At this time, two trellises are pushed onstage for "those who think they have to have scenery." Mrs. Gibbs' garden, he explains, is in the corner of the stage. Next door is the Webbs' house and garden.

It is a nice town, the Stage Manager explains, even though "nobody very remarkable ever came out of it." Tombstone dates, he adds, go back to 1670s and 80s.

The Stage Manager catches sight of Doc Gibbs coming down the street and comments that another day is beginning in "our town." The paper boy is now getting up, and Shorty Hawkins is preparing to flag the 5:45 train for Boston.

Commentary

In this play, Wilder deliberately violates **traditional theatrical devices**. First, he does not use a curtain or reveal a prearranged stage setting. Instead, the Stage Manager provides a few pieces of furniture and begins addressing the audience directly. Although it is true that this particular town is set in New Hampshire, it represents the typical American small town. Viewers can thus imagine any town that they have experienced.

The reader should have a mental picture of what the Stage

Manager looks like. He should be relaxed and low-key, dress quite ordinarily, and resemble a citizen of a small town.

The absence of the typical methods of **exposition** is a marked departure from tradition. Usually, the playwright contrives some scene which reveals to the audience the events which have preceded the immediate action of the play. In this play, the Stage Manager, like the chorus of a Greek drama, supplies a direct link between viewer and action. He is unbound by time or place and speaks of past, present, and future as though they were all of one piece. For this reason, the play lacks **suspense**.

Wilder also breaks with traditional concepts of **dramatic illusion**. In the usual play, the dramatist hopes that the audience will become emotionally involved in imaginary events and will forget the surrounding theater. Wilder makes no effort to convince the audience that the events of the play are real. In fact, he constantly reminds the audience that they are in a theater watching actors perform in a make-believe world. Wilder's purpose is to present, as far as possible, an enactment of a typical day in a small town.

Wilder carefully introduces the houses of the two main families whose actions occupy a major portion of the play. Note that Mr. Webb and Doc Gibbs represent the professions of journalism and medicine.

Summary (Continued)

The Stage Manager gives background information about the families because "in our town we like to know the facts about everybody." As he notices Doc Gibbs coming up Main Street, he tells us something about the Gibbs family. Sometime in the future, he explains, after Doc Gibbs' death in 1930, the new hospital will be named for him. He will live a few years after his wife dies of pneumonia.

Doc Gibbs passes Joe Crowell, Jr., the paper boy, and in answer to Joe's question, the doctor explains that he has been out all night delivering twins over in "Polish Town." The Stage Manager interrupts to explain that Joe Crowell will be one of the brightest boys ever to graduate from Grover's Corners and will be awarded a scholarship to Massachusetts Tech, but that he will be killed in France during the war. All Joe's education will go for nothing.

The Stage Manager then points to Howie Newsome, a man in his thirties wearing overalls, coming down the street in a horse-drawn wagon and delivering milk. He leaves bottles at the Webbs' house, then crosses over to talk to Doc Gibbs. The doctor announces that he has delivered twins to Mrs. Goruslawski.

Mrs. Gibbs enters and calls the children to get up. Howie continues along his milk route. The doctor tells his wife that the birth went as easily as delivering kittens. Mrs. Gibbs, a constant worrier, calls to her children, George and Rebecca, to hurry or be late for school. She chides her husband for trying to work on three hours' sleep and complains that George whines too much and concentrates only on baseball. Rebecca dislikes the blue gingham dress that her mother has ironed. Mrs. Gibbs assures Rebecca that she always looks nice. At Rebecca's complaint that George is throwing soap, their mother threatens to slap both of them.

During the give and take of the Gibbs family breakfast, Mrs. Webb enters and calls her children, Wally and Emily, to hurry or be late for school. They come down for breakfast. The Stage Manager interrupts with the fact that the factory in Grover's Corners makes blankets. Mrs. Webb complains that Wally is studying at the table. Emily announces that she is a bright girl with a wonderful memory. Across the way, Mrs. Gibbs promises George that she will ask Doc about an increase in George's allowance of twenty-five cents a week.

At the sound of the first bell, all of the children charge out of the house and run for school. Then Mrs. Gibbs feeds her chickens from her apron. She and Mrs. Webb string beans. Mrs. Gibbs tells of a second-hand furniture dealer who is offering three-hundred-and-fifty dollars for her heirloom highboy, which is a tall chest of drawers on legs. She would like to sell it and use the money for a trip to Paris, but Doc Gibbs likes to travel only to Civil War battlegrounds. Mrs. Webb encourages her to make the sale.

Commentary

It is apparent that there is no sense of anticipation or plot complication thus far. Instead, Wilder presents a typical day filled with unremarkable details, such as Wally's study of Canada. The one noteworthy event — the birth of twins — suggests that life is a continuing cycle. It has a certain humdrum, repetitious, yet secure routine. For example, Mrs. Gibbs considers spending money on a trip to Paris, but she never goes there — not because she can't, but because European travel does not fit the preconceived pattern of her life.

The attraction of this benign monotony is a mesmerizing flow of days that go on without too much bother by the inhabitants. Its routineness is taken for granted. This theme of predictability appears in the last act when Emily returns to the past to appreciate the simplistic routine of a single day. She realizes then—only after death—that life is a priceless opportunity.

Summary (Continued)

The Stage Manager dismisses the two women and asks Professor Willard to interject some historic data. The professor begins as far back as prehistory with tedious, pedantic details and works his way forward. He misstates the population as 2,640 because he is unaware that Doctor Gibbs has delivered two babies. The Stage Manager then calls on Editor Webb to report the social and economic status of the town. Webb is momentarily delayed because he cut his hand while eating an apple.

During Mr. Webb's account, he notes that Grover's Corners is composed of mostly lower-middle-class people who are eighty-six percent Republican and eighty-five percent Protestant. He concludes that life there must be satisfying because ninety percent of the young people settle in their hometown. When he finishes his comments, the Stage Manager asks if anyone in the audience wants to ask a question. One woman wants to know if there is much drinking. A belligerent man asks if there is any culture in the town. The editor tells them that there is not much drinking and that no one is much concerned about social injustice. Culture, he declares, is limited in Grover's Corners.

The Stage Manager's narrative then jumps forward to early afternoon, as Emily is coming home from school. George hurries to catch up with her. He suggests a communication system from her window to his so that Emily can help him with difficult algebra problems. He freely acknowledges that she is naturally bright. When they reach Emily's home, George leaves for the baseball field. Emily, while joining her mother in stringing beans, asks if her mother thinks Emily is pretty. Mrs. Webb assures Emily that she is pretty enough for normal purposes.

The Stage Manager returns and lists the items that will be enclosed in the cornerstone of the new bank. He intends to include a copy of the play as a message to people a thousand years hence of how residents grew up, married, lived, and died. In the distance the

Congregational Church choir sings "Blessed Be the Tie That Binds."

Meanwhile, two ladders, representing the second stories of the two houses, are moved onstage. George and Emily mount the ladders. George calls to Emily for help with a math problem. She gives him some hints. She also points out how wonderful the moon is.

In the background, Simon Stimson, the choir director, asks how many people can sing at Fred Hersey's wedding. Back at the Gibbses, the doctor calls to George and describes how his mother had to chop firewood because George has been shirking his chores. The doctor promises to increase George's allowance to fifty cents a week because George is getting older. He implies that George must take on more responsibility by helping his mother.

Mrs. Webb and Mrs. Gibbs return from choir practice. Mrs. Soames, who accompanies them, complains about Simon's drinking. Mrs. Gibbs explains that Dr. Ferguson is aware of Simon's dependency, yet keeps him on as organist. The rest of the congregation has little choice but to look the other way.

Mrs. Gibbs returns home. Her husband complains that she is later than usual and accuses her of gossiping. She replies that Simon Stimson was very drunk at choir practice, and that she wonders how long Dr. Ferguson can continue to forgive him. Doc Gibbs, who indicates that he knows the inside details of Simon's problems, observes that some people are not made for small-town life.

At 9:30, Bill Warren, the town constable, comes by and greets Mr. Webb. He notes that Simon Stimson "is rolling around a little." Simon strolls unsteadily down the street; he passes both men without speaking. Mr. Webb asks Bill to help stop George from taking up smoking. The constable says goodnight and departs.

Mr. Webb notices Emily in the upstairs window. He tells her goodnight and goes into the house. Across the way, George Gibbs and his sister are looking out the window. Rebecca comments on the minister's unusual method of addressing a letter to Jane Crofut. Then the Stage Manager appears and announces, "That's the end of the First Act, friends. You can go and smoke now, those that smoke."

Commentary

The reader may be puzzled at Act I. In *Our Town*, each act must be interpreted in terms of the entire play. First, Wilder concerns himself with birth in the first act, marriage in the second act, and death in the final act. Thus, Act I opens with dawn, the birth of the day, as well as the birth of twins. In addition to human birth, Wilder reveals the beginning of a friendship which will develop into marriage. In the guise of the Stage Manager, the playwright becomes a kind of midwife: he delivers each of the main characters as literary creations and symbolic mirrors of the typical boy/girl relationship.

Furthermore, in terms of the whole play, Wilder presents a plea for the viewer to enjoy life to its fullest. In the last act, he notes that most people live their lives without appreciating the small, insignificant moments. These small things later become important when death takes them away. To present this theme, Wilder painstakingly introduces the audience to the seemingly mundane aspects of life. Therefore, the first act presents short scenes from life as entertainment and, more important, as lessons.

These short scenes become especially important to the play as a whole. A review recalls what each scene contributes to the total effect:

- **The first scene presents a paper boy and a milkman. One delivers nourishment for the mind and the other delivers food for the body.**

- **Then, two families, like families everywhere, involve themselves in getting children ready for school.**

- **The third scene shows two mothers conversing. Their friendship represents the kind of support system that flourishes in a small-town environment.**

- **The fourth scene reveals a boy and a girl returning from school. Their walk together suggests the "two-by-two" arrangement which evolves into love and marriage in Act II.**

- **The fifth scene depicts a bright student helping a slower student. In this stereotyped vignette, the brighter student is the girl, who helps an athletic, baseball-minded boy.**

- **The sixth scene shows a father promising to raise his son's allowance but suggesting subtly that the boy help his mother more.**

- The seventh scene depicts choir practice at a Protestant church and the concern of choir members for the organist's alcoholic addiction. In almost every social setting, there are people who drink too much and about whom others gossip.

- The final scene shows these various people retiring for the night. One couple takes a walk to look at the moon. Another person is concerned that his son will take up smoking.

In each scene, the activities represent the normal, day-to-day life of average people. These are the events that comprise human life. They are the facets of living which people take for granted and perform by rote. The older we get, the more we realize the value of these moments—and how little we valued them at the time. After death, they are gone forever. Wilder emphasizes these seemingly insignificant details in order to reverse the usual conception of what is important. Thus, he concludes that it is *not* the momentous events, but the trivialities that become meaningful.

To stress the universality of these events, Wilder sets the stage with no scenery, thereby denying dramatic illusion. Because he forces the viewer to fill in the blanks left by the barren stage, each viewer creates an individualized and detailed mental picture. The words that the characters speak become more significant because they are the *only* source of imagery.

Because Wilder does not build anticipation of events that are to come, the viewer perceives no mysteries to be resolved. Even the matter of Simon Stimson's drinking creates little tension, since the matter is presented mundanely and without alarm. The experience of Act I, ending with a reminder that it is time for smokers to adjourn from the theater, breaks any illusion of traditional drama and reminds the audience that they are not viewing a typical play.

Behind Wilder's emphasis on a bare stage is a subtle understanding of how our minds work during a play. We can imagine any small town. Set on the individual mental stage conjured up in each viewer's mind, the significance of small glimpses of human interaction develops into a major assessment of what makes life worth living. Thus, the audience is left with small, realistic details of life in a small town—in any setting, in any time.

ACT II

Summary

The Stage Manager waits until everyone is seated, then states that three years have passed since Act I. He philosophizes that almost everybody in the world gets married. Act I, he says, was called "Daily Life." This act is called "Love and Marriage." The time of Act II is early morning on July 7, 1904, just after the high school commencement. As in Act I, the 5:45 rumbles through town, bound for Boston.

The stage is about the same. Mrs. Gibbs' garden is on one side and Mrs. Webb's on the other, each drenched with heavy rain. As in the first act, the two women come down to make breakfast in their respective kitchens. In the Stage Manager's assessment of the women's lives: "They brought up two children apiece, washed, cleaned the house—and never a nervous breakdown."

Commentary

Although the Stage Manager did not explain in the first act that it was called "Daily Life," he makes that fact clear at the beginning of Act II. He also reveals that the focus of Act II is love and marriage. To be more specific, the first act featured not only daily life but also birth. He does not give a name for Act III, but he notes, "There's another act coming after this: I reckon you can guess what that's about." Thus, four themes take shape: birth, daily life, marriage, and death.

In Act I, Joe Crowell, Jr., complains that his teacher is getting married. Later, Simon Stimson mentions Jane Trowbridge's marriage as he prepares the choir for Fred Hersey's wedding. This triple reference to matrimony prepares the audience for the union of George and Emily, which is central to Act II. Likewise, the observation that "most everybody in the world climbs into their graves married" leads directly to the theme of Act III.

This intermingling of focus emphasizes an important aspect of the play: the lives of the characters cannot be dissected into single moments in which birth, love, marriage, and death are the *only* factors to be considered. Rather, the interweaving of the themes comprises the fabric of community life. At any one time, these concepts interplay, reflecting on each other in myriad ways.

Occasionally, the Stage Manager interrupts or adds some detail that is especially memorable. In one speech, he describes how the two housewives have each fulfilled the usual duties of a wife and mother and never had a nervous breakdown. He implies that perhaps life in a small town is not beset with as many difficulties and neuroses as life in metropolitan areas. Another interpretation of Wilder's italics suggests that stereotypical "woman's work" at the turn of the century was predictable, repetitious, and not without its hazards.

Wilder's central concept takes a more definite shape in Act II. The Stage Manager makes loose reference to a line by an unnamed poet (actually Edgar Lee Masters, author of "Lucinda Matlock"): "You've got to love life to have life, and you've got to have life to love life." This idea develops into a significant statement in the last act—the need to appreciate all aspects of existence. The Stage Manager's comment about how the details form a "vicious cycle" prepares the viewer for the anguish experienced by the dead in Act III.

Summary (Continued)

While Mrs. Gibbs and Mrs. Webb prepare breakfast, Howie Newsome delivers milk. Si Crowell, Joe Crowell's younger brother, appears with the morning paper. Si worries that Grover's Corners is losing its best baseball pitcher—George Gibbs. Si doesn't understand how George can give up baseball just to get married. Constable Warren enters to check the drain pipes. There has been heavy rainfall; he fears flooding. Howie thinks the weather will clear up.

Mrs. Gibbs orders extra milk and cream because she expects a houseful of relatives. Across the street, Mrs. Webb also orders more milk and cream than usual. Howie expresses confidence that the newlyweds will be happy. Both women urge Howie and his wife to come to the wedding.

Doc Gibbs appears and comments to his wife that she is losing one of her chicks. Mrs. Gibbs feels like crying and insists that George and Emily are too young for marriage. Doc Gibbs reminds her of their own wedding day and his fear of matrimony. Mrs. Gibbs concludes that the natural order of human relationships is "two by two." He continues his reminiscence of how he worried that they would run out of things to talk about and have to eat in silence. But for twenty years, he muses, they have had plenty of topics to discuss.

George comes down for breakfast and nervously jokes about

losing his freedom, which he symbolizes by pretending to cut his own throat. He starts across the yard to see Emily, but his mother, mindful of her role as chief worrier, makes him come back and put on his overshoes.

George's appearance perturbs Emily's mother, who explains that he must not bring bad luck by seeing the bride on her wedding day. George asks Mr. Webb if he believes that old superstition. Mr. Webb declares that there is often common sense behind superstitions. Mrs. Webb goes upstairs to keep Emily from coming down. As she leaves, she tells George to have a cup of coffee before going home.

Mr. Webb tries to discuss life and marriage with his future son-in-law. George wishes that a person could get married without so much bother, but Mr. Webb explains that it has always been like this because women want to "make sure that the knot's tied in a mighty public way." Mr. Webb relates the advice he received from his father about how to maintain control of women. He adds that he ignored the advice and concludes that George should not solicit advice on personal matters.

Mrs. Webb returns and sends George home so that Emily can come down to breakfast. Mr. Webb makes up another old saying: "No bridegroom should see his father-in-law on the day of the wedding."

Commentary

Even though Act II is entitled "Love and Marriage," Wilder again arranges a routine of commonplace activities within the framework of daily life. In other words, he is repeating many of the activities found in the first act, except for the notable addition of French toast to the breakfast menu. Both the first and second acts begin with the appearance of the milkman and paper boy. Both characters discuss trivialities, such as the weather. The repetition gives an added air of realism to the scene. It makes life in "our town" seem more familiar, more predictable.

In Act II, however, these typical events occur on a wedding day. A young boy cannot understand why his high school hero can give up baseball in order to marry. The father of the groom teases the mother and reminds her of their own wedding day. The father remembers how nervous she was before they married. The mother worries that the couple are too young and that the new wife may not be capable of taking care of her son as she, the mother, has done in the past.

Mrs. Gibbs feels the need to mother George for the last time. In the name of good health, she bosses him, making him return to put on overshoes. As a means of freeing him from her control, she promises that in the future he can do as he pleases.

As a part of the prenuptial scene, Wilder has his characters discuss standard superstitions concerning weddings. He implies that old-fashioned beliefs have a basis in common sense without actually explaining them. Finally, Mr. Webb points out that people rarely pay attention to advice.

In general, Wilder tries to include anecdotal, Norman Rockwell-style activities connected with the humor and traditional elements that accompany a wedding. In this way, he evokes a sense of its importance, even though one wedding does not differ demonstrably from another.

Summary (Continued)

The Stage Manager interrupts to reflect on how the relationship between George and Emily began. His reason is that "suddenly you are young and you make a decision to get married and the next thing you know you are seventy and that whitehaired lady at your side has eaten over fifty thousand meals with you."

The Stage Manager explains that George has just been elected president of the senior class for the next year and that Emily has been elected secretary-treasurer. Emily is walking down main street carrying an armful of schoolbooks. George catches up with her and asks to carry her books. He says that he is awfully glad she was elected.

Suddenly George asks why she is angry with him. Emily gives an honest answer: George has changed during the last year; he spends too much time playing baseball, and people talk about him because he doesn't speak to anyone and acts conceited. George stammers, then admits that Emily's honesty is beneficial because "it's hard for a fella not to have faults creep into his character." Emily explains that she wants men to be perfect and there is no reason why George shouldn't be. George maintains that "men aren't naturally good; but girls are." He asks her to have an ice cream soda with him.

George and Emily enter Morgan's drugstore. The Stage Manager appears in the role of Mr. Morgan, the druggist. He notices that Emily has been crying. George fibs that Emily has been frightened by Tom

Huckins' maniac driving. George insists that they order two strawberry ice cream sodas to celebrate their election.

After being served, George exclaims that he is glad to have a friend who will tell him all the things "that ought to be told me." Emily regrets having said anything because she sees that her statement is not true.

George asks her to write him when he goes away to agriculture college. She promises to do so but wonders if he will still be interested in Grover's Corners. He admits that he sees no *real* need for going away. He has talked with farmers who see no necessity for a farmer to attend agricultural college. Furthermore, Uncle Luke is almost ready to retire and let George take over the farm. Suddenly, George decides not to go to college. He plans to tell his father that night.

George then warms to Emily, asserting that she was wrong in one aspect of her criticism. He assures her that he has always noticed her. Whenever he plays ball, he looks to see if she is in the bleachers. He has tried to walk home with her, but she always seems to be with someone else. Suddenly, he wonders if, upon his improvement, Emily will consent to be . . . Emily interrupts that, yes, she is already and always has been.

George tells Emily that it is really good that they had this little talk. He asks Mr. Morgan to wait until he can run home to get the money to pay their bill. He offers his watch as surety for the debt.

Commentary

This is the central scene of Act II. It presents the simple but appealing account of how two teenagers overcome a misunderstanding and disclose their mutual love. The success of the scene lies in Wilder's ability to re-create a romantic scene without cluttering it with sentiment. The scene is both honest and slightly nostalgic, but it contains hints of the absurdity of youthful declarations of love. The scene is delicately balanced between tenderness and the almost comic quality found in the young people's naivete.

In terms of the entire play, this is a love that grows out of daily life and leads to a sensible, down-to-earth union of two people from the same background. George, who is easily out-maneuvered by Emily's logic and poise, makes up a clumsy ruse to cover for her tears. His manly protection of his girl from a maniac driver presages his moving farewell at Emily's grave in Act III. Even though George fills the role of a loyal, protective husband, he is unable to hold back death.

Summary (Continued)

The Stage Manager removes his spectacles, claps his hands, and begins the wedding scene, in which he plays the role of minister. He comments that everything about a wedding cannot be represented, so he will include only a few details. As clergyman, he speaks about weddings in general and repeats Mrs. Gibbs' statement that "people were made to live two-by-two." The hero of this scene, he assures the audience, is nature. From marriages come more people and "every child born into the world is nature's attempt to make a perfect human being."

Handel's "Largo" begins, the guests take their seats on the pews, and church bells sound. Mrs. Webb stops on the way to her seat and blurts out to the audience that it is terrible to send young girls into the cruel world without their knowing anything about marriage. She hopes that some of Emily's friends have enlightened her about what to expect.

Three of George's baseball teammates pass by and whistle and catcall to him, teasing him about his sexual innocence. The Stage Manager intercedes and good-naturedly pushes the boys offstage. He apologizes by saying that since Roman times there has been a lot of off-color innuendo connected with weddings, but now Grover's Corners is more civilized. "So they say," he adds.

As the choir sings "Love Divine, All Love Excelling," George arrives and withdraws from the congregation. His mother goes to him. He tells her that he does not want to get old. Mrs. Gibbs sternly admonishes him for shaming her. They trade roles, with George comforting her and promising to bring Emily each Thursday night for dinner.

Meanwhile Emily appears dressed in traditional white. She calls to her "papa," who leaves his seat and advances toward her. She frightens him by expressing her dislike for George and her desire to go off with her father. She reminds him of how he used to say she was his girl. Mr. Webb calls George over and formally hands over his daughter. George and Emily embrace. The march from *Lohengrin* sounds. The wedding begins.

Mrs. Soames, a wedding guest, drowns out the couple's vows with shrill comments on the loveliness of the wedding. The minister ponders the two hundred couples he has married, who follow the pattern of home, family, approaching old age, and death. George and Emily exit to Mendelssohn's "Wedding March." The Stage Manager notes, "That's all the Second Act, folks."

Commentary

When the stage manager speaks about the wedding, he tells the audience that he cannot include every detail. He chooses the most appropriate aspects and leaves the rest to the viewers' imaginations. This technique is a miniature of Wilder's approach to the whole play. He takes a few isolated events and universalizes them. The resulting scene is typical of weddings the world over—the nervous bride and groom, sympathetic parents, suggestive wedding jests, and benign comments from idealistic wedding guests.

For George and Emily, the wedding is the high point of their lives. For the viewer, however, it is just another small-town wedding with nothing to set it apart from other similar ceremonies. Mrs. Soames, who is the gushy type, makes heartfelt comments about the loveliness of the event, but her glowing remarks fail to convince the audience that there is anything unique about this particular wedding. As the minister concludes, "Once in a thousand times it's interesting."

In Wilder's view of life, nature is the key factor in Act II. As he observes, people are born, grow up, marry, and then die. Thus marriage is a part of the natural order of things—a logical development in the process of living. Earlier, he spoke of the usual tendency of people to live by twos. Consequently, following the birth motif of Act I, the pairing of Emily and George follows quite naturally as the central image of Act II.

Mrs. Webb bemoans the fact that Emily knows so little of life. Her remarks prove prophetic in Act III, when Emily dies as a result of childbirth. Yet, the evolution of Emily's love for George, whom she has known all her life, seems a natural outgrowth of their childhood friendship, both to the young people and their parents. The tragedy of Emily's death is, like the joy of marriage, just a part of the life process.

It also seems natural that potential brides and grooms on the verge of matrimony experience last-minute hesitations—even though their love is well-founded. Wilder deftly works into this scene some of George's and Emily's last-minute fears. Both suddenly realize that they are exiting childhood, a time when they felt secure in parental warmth and protection. They pause before taking the final step into maturity. Yet, when they see each other, love pushes them over the threshold. At the end of the scene, Mrs. Soames' inane chatter drowns out the ceremony. The wedding is condensed into the single vow from George, "I do."

Winding up the scene, the Stage Manager comments that he, as a minister, has joined thousands of couples. He notes that millions of marriages have taken place. Wilder causes us to see this wedding as a commonplace event—a single episode in a long series of matings. As he sums up, "The cottage, the go-cart, the Sunday-afternoon drives in the Ford, the first rheumatism, the grandchildren, the second rheumatism, the death-bed, the reading of the will—." The natural progression seems unstoppable.

Wilder's insistence on the rightness of marriage as a normal, commonplace expectation of life blends with the next act, in which he shows the importance of trivial things against the background of death, the natural conclusion of life.

Again, the Stage Manager breaks with the tradition of dramatic illusion by announcing an intermission.

ACT III

Summary

During intermission, stagehands rearrange the stage. They place ten or twelve chairs in three rows. As Act III is about to begin, the audience sees actors take their places in the chairs, leaving an empty chair in the center of the front row beside Mrs. Gibbs and Simon Stimson.

The Stage Manager describes the gradual alteration that has occurred in Grover's Corners over the past nine years. He stresses that "on the whole, things don't change much around here." He introduces the scene, a graveyard on a beautiful, windy hilltop on the outskirts of town, which is "certainly an important part of Grover's Corners."

The Stage Manager reminds us that the characters are friends—Mrs. Gibbs, Mr. Stimson, Mrs. Soames, and Wally Webb. Many residents have brought other loved ones to the hill and left them. Some day, everyone will come to the cemetery to stay when their "fit's [fight's] over."

He notes that there is something eternal about human life. The nice thing about the dead is that they lose interest in the living. Their pleasures and ambitions cease as they wean themselves away from earthly concerns and wait quietly and peacefully for something to happen—something that will clarify the eternal part of them. The stage manager warns that the comments of the spirits may offend because the dead have different concerns from the living.

Commentary

Unlike the former acts, the third act moves outside of town to the cemetery, which commands an inspiring view of surrounding lakes, mountains, and towns. The audience observes first-hand the changing of the sparse scenery. The players sit quietly, but without stiffness. They speak matter-of-factly and without sentimentality or mournfulness.

The Stage Manager reports that Grover's Corners has changed little. The emphasis is upon death as an accepted part of town life. Just as people are born with little fanfare in Act I, they depart from life in the same fashion in Act III. The appearance of Mrs. Soames links the end of Act II to the beginning of Act III. Just as she is a member of the church choir and a player in the wedding scene, her life reaches its end and she now appears among the other spirits.

Wilder here addresses not only death, but his view on immortality. He speaks of the "something" in each human being that is eternal, yet he gives the "something" no name. In explanation of the human lack of familiarity with this unnamed element, he emphasizes that people are aware of certain things, but we "don't take'm out and look at'm very often." By refraining from using the word "soul," he leaves the interpretation open. The playwright indicates that the spirits await a momentous happening, but he gives no clue as to the nature of the event. Perhaps they anticipate a day of judgment, another life, or a complete withdrawal into peace and tranquility.

Finally, the playwright suggests that death frees human beings from all the petty, insignificant annoyances which haunt the living. "The dead don't stay interested in us living people for very long. Gradually, gradually, they lose . . . the ambitions they had." They also separate themselves from pleasure, suffering, and most of the memories of their earthly lives.

At the end of this introduction, the viewers see a newly dug grave being prepared for an unnamed person.

Summary (Continued)

After the Stage Manager ends his introductory speech, we see Emily's cousin, Sam Craig, enter and address the undertaker, Joe Stoddard, who is supervising Emily's grave. Sam introduces himself because he moved to Buffalo twelve years earlier. He notices Mrs. Gibbs' grave and recalls the fact that his Aunt Julia is dead.

While Joe and Sam talk, Mrs. Gibbs' spirit identifies Sam for the rest of the dead. Mr. Stimson says he always feels uncomfortable when the living visit the cemetery. Meanwhile, Joe wonders if the dead chose the verses which appear on the tombstones. He reads Simon Stimson's epitaph and recalls that Simon committed suicide. The epitaph is only a few notes of music which Simon chose before taking his life.

Sam asks about Emily's death and learns that she died during childbirth. Joe adds: "'Twas her second, though. There's a little boy 'bout four years old." The Gibbs lot is almost full; Emily's grave is in a new section that has just opened by Avenue B.

While Sam and Joe talk, four men enter from the left carrying a casket. Others follow in procession under an umbrella. Mrs. Soames wonders who the new person is. Mrs. Gibbs replies that it is her daughter-in-law, Emily, who died giving birth. Mrs. Soames says that she remembers childbirth and how awful life was, but after a pause she notes softly how wonderful it was too. Simon Stimson disagrees. Mrs. Soames then recalls the loveliness of Emily and George's wedding, how smart Emily was as a high school student, and the beauty of George and Emily's new farm.

Emily, wearing a white dress and girlishly long hair tied with a ribbon, emerges from the crowd of mourners. Hesitant and a little dazed, she approaches the other spirits. With quiet dignity and serenity, she greets them. They return her greeting.

Emily expresses the newness she is experiencing. It seems to her that she has been apart from the living for thousands of years. She dislikes being new in the cemetery. She tells "Mother Gibbs" what a wonderful place she and George made of their farm, but Mrs. Gibbs takes little interest in her human endeavors. Emily adds that the farm won't be the same to George now that she is dead. Suddenly she realizes that living people don't understand death. She tells Mr. Carter that her little boy is spending the day at his house. Like Mrs. Gibbs, Mr. Carter seems uninterested in human affairs.

Emily is curious to know when her feelings of connection with the living will cease. Mrs. Gibbs replies that she must be patient. As the funeral service ends, various mourners begin to leave the stage. Emily notices that Father Gibbs places some of the funeral flowers on Mrs. Gibbs' grave. One of the spirits comments on the change in the weather.

Suddenly, Emily sits up. She realizes that she can return to the living world and relive all her days. The Stage Manager, however, as well as Mrs. Soames and Mrs. Gibbs all advise against returning to the past. They assure her that she will be disappointed. The Stage Manager adds that she not only will live in the past but also will see herself living it. Thus, as she watches, she will be able to remain in the present while knowing the future.

Mrs. Gibbs tries to dissuade Emily. The point of living among the dead, she says, is to forget the past and think of what lies ahead. Emily, however, insists on seeing for herself. Mrs. Gibbs advises her to choose an unimportant day. Emily compromises by choosing to relive her twelfth birthday.

Commentary

In this section, Wilder demonstrates the difference between the living and the dead. Obviously, the presence of the living makes the spirits uncomfortable. They purposely try to forget the living and prepare themselves for something that is to occur in the future.

In the first two acts, Wilder employs several techniques to familiarize the audience with background material, most frequently by having the Stage Manager supply data. By Act III, however, Wilder expresses larger, more significant ideas through the Stage Manager and saves exposition for minor actors. He uses a traditional device: he has a citizen of the town talk to a man who has been away for twelve years. As the returnee asks questions and catches up with his family and the town, the audience learns pertinent facts.

By having Emily appear as one of the newly dead, Wilder can express her newly formed thoughts about metamorphosis from farm wife and mother to spirit. Without a new arrival as a stimulus, the older spirits would not have reason to discuss their thoughts on being dead. Another reason for Emily's importance is that she has been a key player in the drama all along. Therefore, to place her among the dead gives the drama a tighter structure by holding the focus on her.

Because Emily wears a white dress and a youthful hair style, she evokes her joyous departure from Act II as George's bride. Thus, Wilder blends the two acts, thereby emphasizing the innocence and femininity of his main character.

Mrs. Soames, a minor character, again performs an important function. She is the spirit who best remembers Emily's wedding, thereby connecting or relating the two acts even more firmly to each other. With her outspoken **romanticism,** Mrs. Soames also sums up life – both its wonderful and awful qualities. In contrast to Mrs. Soames' **idealism** is the negative view of Simon Stimson, who committed suicide because of his alcoholism. Apparently, Wilder chooses to abstain from moralizing on the type of life which Mr. Stimson lived or the reasons that he takes issue with Mrs. Soames' blatant rhapsodizing.

Wilder emphasizes that the dead form a unique family, free from the toil, struggle, and conflict that plagues life. Ironically, it is the living rather than those in coffins who are "sort of shut up in little boxes." Even though the dead sit quietly without moving, they exude a sense of freedom through their voices and their serenity. In contrast to their peace, the living constantly combat troubles. Wilder indicates that most people are so weighted down with life's troubles that they are unable to appreciate the simple fact that they are *alive.* Emily has yet to make this discovery.

Because the spirits plead with Emily not to relive her past, the audience is prepared for her terrible disappointment in the next scene. Since Emily is able to live in the present and see the future, she will understand the futility and misunderstanding which clouds human life.

Summary (Continued)

The Stage Manager tells Emily that she can go back to Tuesday, February 11, 1899. He reminds her of the events that occurred just before her birthday. Her father was returning on the early-morning train after having been away for several days in Clinton, New York, to make a speech at Hamilton College, his alma mater.

The scene opens on the town as it was. Emily delights in memorable landmarks, but expresses surprise to see Howie Newsome and Constable Bill Warren because she knows that they are now dead. It is early morning and the milkman, paper boy, and constable appear on the streets. The constable reports saving a man from freezing to death in the snow.

Emily's mother calls the children to breakfast. Emily is surprised at how young her mother looks. She overhears trivial conversation. Her parents discuss Mr. Webb's trip as well as Emily's birthday. More in wonder than grief, Emily cries out: "I can't bear it. They're so young and beautiful. Why did they ever have to get old? . . . I can't look at everything hard enough."

Emily comes downstairs; her mother remonstrates: "Birthday or no birthday, I want you to eat your breakfast good and slow." Emily's reply is filled with emotion: "Oh, Mama, just look at me one minute as though you really saw me . . ." Emily's mother gives her a birthday gift and describes her brother's gift. Then Emily hears her father's voice calling her.

Suddenly, she turns to the Stage Manager and tells him that the scene is unbearable. "I can't go on. It goes so fast. We don't have time to look at one another." She asks the Stage Manager to take her back "up the hill—to my grave." As she leaves, she says: "Oh, earth, you're too wonderful for anybody to realize you." Then she asks the Stage Manager: "Do any human beings ever realize life while they live it?—every, every minute?" The Stage Manager tells her no, but suggests that some saints and poets do value life.

By now it is dark. The dead enjoy the companionship of the stars. George Gibbs approaches Emily's grave and falls full length across it at Emily's feet. Emily looks at Mrs. Gibbs and remarks: "They don't understand, do they?"

The Stage Manager returns and reports that almost everybody is asleep in Grover's Corners. The stars are shining brightly, but scholars say that there is no life on other stars. Here on earth, everyone strains to make something of life. "The strain's so bad that every sixteen hours everybody lies down and gets a rest." He looks at his watch. It is eleven o'clock. He pauses, then suggests that the audience go home to get some rest.

Commentary

Emily's return to life is a structural device which unites the action of the play. The fact that the audience witnesses the same setting that opened Act I gives the play continuity and familiarity. The comments and actions of people mirror the commonplace actions of the first scenes. This repetition forces the audience to see through Emily's eyes the replay of her past. Therefore, it is easier to comprehend her disillusionment as she hurriedly returns to her place on the hill.

The final scene expresses most clearly Wilder's focus. The earth is a place where everything happens and everything is important. The playwright impels the audience toward an understanding and appreciation of life's brevity. A subtle reminder of how quickly life can end is contained in the constable's rescue of a man from death by freezing. Returned to girlhood, Emily concludes that her mother is so busy with housewifely details that she takes no time to appreciate the wonder of her family. Emily's impassioned cry to her mother that they should look at each other underscores the human inability to absorb the essence of living while it is going on.

Wistfully, Emily, who is only twenty-six at the time of her death, realizes that she is out of place in the familiar scene. She bids farewell to ticking clocks, sunflowers, food and coffee, new-ironed dresses, hot baths, sleeping and waking. Still, with all that she has experienced since the beginning of Act I, she seems to have aged very little from her first appearance onstage, even though she has progressed from schoolgirl to wife and mother.

Overall, the scene focuses on human frailty, which keeps people from enjoying all the good that life has to offer. Overcome with dismay at earthly wastefulness, Emily comprehends that the living are blind to everyday wonders. Perhaps, as Wilder states, saints and poets do realize some of every moment of life, but the average person allows these precious trifles to pass by without recognizing their worth.

Simon sums up human faults more harshly than Emily. To him the living move in a "cloud of ignorance . . . at the mercy of one self-centered passion, or another." Perhaps he is bitter because he wasted his own life on alcohol. He recognizes that he "trampled on the feelings" of others. Consequently, he feels that life was a terrible experience. The other spirits acknowledge that Simon's summation contains a kernel of truth, but they insist that life had good points.

At the end of the scene, George comes to mourn Emily's death. Apparently he is immobilized by deep grief. Still, as much as Emily loved her husband in life, she has changed since her death. Dispassionately, she looks at him without sharing his grief and comments: "They don't understand." Emily comprehends fully a fact that George has yet to learn – that death frees the living from their earthly troubles and conflicts.

The final appearance of the Stage Manager reminds the audience that the cycle is complete. In passing, he mentions how the residents of this little star that is the world, strain to achieve their potential. Pointedly, he winds his watch, thereby breaking the spell and realigning the audience with the normal passage of time. Yet his final remark again allies the viewers with the citizens of Grover's Corners, each of whom needs a "good rest." The simplicity of his departure is in keeping with his overall purpose – to guide the audience through an unassuming but profoundly moving consideration of what it means to be alive.

CHARACTER ANALYSES

EMILY WEBB GIBBS

Emily Webb, who later becomes Mrs. George Gibbs, carries most of the play's meaning. In the opening scenes, she is entering young womanhood. The brightest student in her school, she is very much aware of her good qualities. At sixteen, she is at a stage of life where she concentrates on looks and appearance. Yet Emily maintains a certain winsome sweetness that allows the viewer to accept her high evaluation of herself.

In her conversation with George, Emily displays a normal teenage tendency toward romanticism. By the end of Act I, she sniffs the heliotrope next door and stares pensively at the stars. This early view of Emily prepares the audience for her role in Act III when she discovers that most people don't take the time to examine the act of living. Also, her awareness of mystery in the heavens leads directly to her reappearance as a spirit.

Emily's character is best revealed in Act II when she and George discover love. Emily is an idealist. She wants George to be the best that he can be. She expresses annoyance at him for devoting his time to baseball and neglecting his friends. In other words, Emily feels slighted.

She is explicit in her criticism of George. Her frankness, however, results from disappointment rather than vindictiveness. As soon as George divulges his love for her, Emily regrets criticizing him. By the end of the scene, Emily has reversed her opinion. As soon as she knows that she is truly George's love interest, she loses or represses her feelings of superiority. She is willing to take the subservient role that is typical of both her mother and future mother-in-law.

At the wedding, Emily experiences qualms about starting a new life with George. She seems to fulfill her mother's fears that she is too naive to become a wife. Emily—who misinterprets her apprehension as hatred of George—urges her "papa" to take her away. Her function in the wedding scene is to suggest the universal terror that brides sometimes undergo. In the end, however, she disengages herself from her father's protection and establishes a reliance on her future husband.

Emily's chief function is reserved for Act III. After dying in childbirth and leaving behind a four-year-old son, she hesitantly joins the spirits in the cemetery. She cannot accept her position at first, and being new, she is able to comment on the relative difference between the living and dead. Of the living, she says: "They're sort of shut up in little boxes." Thus, part of her function is to note the irony that she, recently buried in a hillside grave, knows more freedom than the living, who are confined and unjoined to other living beings.

When Emily asks to relive a day in her life, she assists the Stage Manager in speaking Wilder's philosophy concerning the meaning of life and living. During this day, she realizes that the living are so involved in performing commonplace tasks that they take no time to gain a balanced perception of the acts that they perform. They are burdened with troubles and earthly concerns to the point that they miss the ecstasy of the moment. As Emily asks the Stage Manager, "Do human beings ever realize life while they live it?" Apparently, it is not until death that people comprehend that every moment of life is wonderful but that most people fail to relish the experience.

In the final scene, Emily, who has loved George very deeply, has attained a detachment and serenity that the living do not possess. She can therefore observe George's grief without any of the passion of the living. She simply comments that the living don't understand. Thus, Wilder uses Emily as an example of how the average person can live, marry, and die before comprehending the potential of life.

GEORGE GIBBS

If George is not the "all-American" boy, he at least represents the typical American boy. In the first scenes, he is scolded for throwing soap at his sister. Even though he does not deserve it, he wangles a raise in his allowance. Later, he has difficulty with algebra. He uses his boyish charms to convince his intelligent neighbor, Emily, to help him. His invention of a communication system between their houses assures him that help is close at hand.

Later, in Act II, George—Si Crowell's personal hero—is elected president of his senior class. It is likely that his selection is based on superficial traits—such as his prowess on the pitching mound or his personality—rather than his intellectual excellence or leadership qualities. Thus, his inclination toward rowdiness, his love of the all-American game of baseball, and his position as class officer characterize him as the stereotypical small-town American boy.

Also predictable is the fact that he is obsessed with baseball to the exclusion of friends. His thoughts, however, have not strayed completely from Emily. He has thought about her enough to realize the depth of his attraction to her. The drugstore scene captures the emotion of high school students exploring love. To heighten the poignance of the scene, Wilder breaks the spell abruptly so that George can hurry home to get money to pay the bill.

George's ambition and desire to skip college in order to take over his uncle's farm suggest a certain practicality, although current thought might indicate that he is reaching for short-term goals at the expense of long-term preparation for a richer, more secure life. Later, the scenes before the wedding capture the immaturity of young grooms. Fortunately, George's fears of growing old are temporary. As soon as he sees Emily, he recognizes the strength of his love for her and willingly plunges into adulthood.

George's role in the last act is small, yet intensely effective. He has succeeded as a farmer. Coming at night to Emily's grave, he demonstrates his deep and sincere love for her. By throwing himself abjectly across the newly dug grave, he expresses without words his devotion to the woman who has been the center of his life.

George functions in the play as a representative American. In Act I, rather than create a distinct individual, Wilder spotlights traits characteristic of youth in general. Even as an adult, George is an ordinary man performing ordinary tasks. Yet, with one silent action, he rises to a respectable height in Act III by his moving response to Emily's death.

EDITOR CHARLES WEBB

Mr. Webb, a forthright, intelligent man, is a leading citizen of Grover's Corners. Proof lies in the fact that he has been asked back to his alma mater to deliver a speech. He helps the Stage Manager by providing additional background data about the town. His interests lie in the appreciation of nature and the study of history, particularly the life of Napoleon.

Mr. Webb, like his enthusiastic daughter, is never apathetic. As a father, he concerns himself with the possibility that his son has taken up smoking and comforts Emily before she departs from his care to assume the role of wife. As an editor, he acts the part of town booster by stressing Constable Warren's quick thinking in saving a citizen from freezing to death. Still, Mr. Webb seems unperturbed by the fact that Grover's Corners lacks cultural aspirations beyond its appreciation of *Robinson Crusoe,* the Bible, Handel's "Largo," and Whistler's "Mother."

Mr. Webb also functions as a speaker of homespun philosophy and bits of wry humor, such as his remark that the town drunks are "always having remorses every time an evangelist comes to town." On the day of his daughter's wedding, he faces the task of talking man-to-man with his future son-in-law. He creates a witty twist on the notion that the groom should not see the bride before the wedding. His version states that the future father-in-law should not be left alone with the groom.

DOCTOR FRANK GIBBS

Like Mr. Webb, Doc Gibbs represents the professions and functions as just another citizen helping to give believability and realism to the street scene. In Act I, Dr. Gibbs introduces the concept of birth by his announcement that he has just delivered the Goruslawski twins. An opinionated man, he takes an active interest in his son's ambition to be a farmer and smirks at Mrs. Fairchild's citified notions that doors should be locked against burglars.

Like his counterpart, Doc Gibbs takes a keen interest in history. His wife says he is never so happy as when he visits Antietam and Gettysburg, "stopping at every bush and pacing it all out." He is a master of child psychology in his handling of George's laxness at home. By doubling the boy's allowance, he puts the burden on George to earn his fifty cents per week by being more helpful to his mother.

It is quite realistic that the doctor concerns himself with others' troubles, such as Joe Crowell's knee, Mrs. Wentworth's stomach, and Simon Stimson's alcoholism. He dominates his wife with a light hand, makes light of her participation in the church choir, and ignores her dutiful attempts to get him to rest after his late-night obstetrical call. Yet long after her death, he pays tribute to her with a handful of flowers.

MRS. JULIA GIBBS AND MRS. MYRTLE WEBB

These women function in a role similar to that of Doc Gibbs in that they flesh out the picture of the small town. Involved in motherhood roles of getting their children fed and off to school, they relax, share the chore of stringing beans, and discuss Mrs. Gibbs' desire to sell her grandmother's highboy and use the money for a trip to Paris. Both belong to the Congregational Church choir, and both are concerned over the organist's alcoholism.

Wilder offers no more description of these women than he does for any of the other characters. Mrs. Webb is simply "a thin, crisp woman." The playwright takes advantage of stereotyping the women in order to comment that the average woman living in a small town is healthy. "They brought up two children apiece, washed, cleaned the house . . . both of those ladies cooked three meals a day – one of 'em for twenty years, the other for forty – and no summer vacation . . . and never a nervous breakdown." Thus, Wilder implies that small town life is healthful.

As parents, both women take an interest in nutrition and good health practices, such as proper chewing of food and firm posture. Mrs. Gibbs nags Doc Gibbs about working without adequate rest. Mrs. Webb declares, "I'd rather have my children healthy than bright." On the day of the wedding, Mrs. Gibbs insists that George wear overshoes, and Mrs. Webb insists that Emily eat her breakfast.

In the end, Mrs. Gibbs plays a fuller role as mother in that she serves as a protective spirit when Emily first arrives among the dead. Mrs. Gibbs learns that her $350 legacy helped make George and Emily's farm a success, but her primary interest as a spirit is in helping Emily develop the patience to look forward to what comes next.

THE STAGE MANAGER

The Stage Manager is Wilder's unique, multi-purpose invention—a part which he himself played on the stage many times. The Stage Manager functions in opposition to the traditional attempt of drama to convince the audience that it is a part of the action onstage. Instead, Wilder has the Stage Manager come to the edge of the stage to remind the audience directly that they are viewers—not participants. At times he helps move scenery and even interacts with members of the audience. But his presence permeates every scene, whether he speaks as himself or through the persona of the druggist or minister.

The Stage Manager's first and most obvious function is to provide **exposition** of background facts. Traditional exposition occurs when characters reveal facts about place, setting, and plot involvement. Wilder, in defiance of classic method, has the Stage Manager introduce the town and characters. As leader and spokesman, the Stage Manager familiarizes the audience with various aspects of Grover's Corners. Because of his godlike **omniscience**, he is able to move about freely, ignoring the usual confines of time and space. Perhaps more important, he impels the viewer toward Emily. Also, he assists Emily in returning to life to relive a single day.

From this point on, the Stage Manager's function becomes more complex. He assists the audience in judging the action and evaluating relationships. Without his lecturing and commentary, the viewer, lacking forceful emotion or high drama, is in danger of overlooking the significance among so many minor details. In this way, he becomes an instructor, imparting lessons as a part of Wilder's **didactic purpose**.

Besides these functions, the Stage Manager serves as an actor. He steps into scenes and interacts with other players. By departing from his job as master of ceremonies and matter-of-factly assuming the role of Mr. Morgan, Mrs. Forrest, or the minister, he retains his humanity. Because Wilder avoids elevating the Stage Manager above the other characters, he makes him a believable outgrowth of town life, on a par with any other citizen of Grover's Corners.

Finally, the Stage Manager speaks the playwright's thoughts and projects his themes directly. When a question arises, the Stage Manager is there to answer it. When Emily has a problem, the Stage Manager is able to solve it for her and for the audience as well. Whatever wisdom Wilder wants to express beyond the dialogue of the play, he puts into the mouth of the Stage Manager. Through this invention of the Stage Manager, the viewer discovers the value of the humblest of everyday transactions. The Stage Manager demonstrates that "an absolute reality can only be inner, very inner." Thus, he functions as the most important actor, as well as a structural element of the play, and also as a facilitator of each theme.

CRITICAL ESSAYS

THEMATIC STRUCTURE

Our Town violates most of the traditions of the theater. There are no complex **characters** who lend themselves to psychological analysis. The **setting** is the barest minimum. There is virtually no **plot**; consequently no suspense, expectation, or anticipation. Why, then, is the play so popular? Wilder gives some clue in his evaluation: "The response we make when we 'believe' a work of the imagination is that of saying: 'This is the way things are. I have always known it without being fully aware that I knew it. Now in the presence of this play or novel or poem [or picture or piece of music] I know that I know it.'" Thus, by his selectivity, by his ability to *universalize* scenes, and by his basic *humanism*, Wilder offers something with which the viewer can identify.

Many critics believe the play remains popular because of these humanistic ideas—particularly, Wilder's plea for the appreciation of the moment. His basic **theme** emerges from the structuring of the three acts, which interweave the stages of life. As the playwright once wrote: "The central theme of the play . . . is the relation between the countless unimportant details of our daily life, on the one hand, and the great perspective of time, social history and current religious ideas." Consequently, one of Wilder's purposes is to present events of temporary importance against the perspective of eternity.

Act I dwells on the commonplace. It emphasizes dawn, birth, and the beginning of a young love that will develop into marriage in the second act. All of the scenes in Act I depict some trivial, predictable activity. Later, the full significance of these minor details becomes clear. As Wilder points out, most people live the first act of their lives without relishing the pricelessness of inconsequential encounters, such as greeting townspeople, getting an education, or eating breakfast with family members.

Act II presents the second cycle of daily life in a town. People grow up and marry. Thus love and marriage, a natural phenomenon which perpetuates the human race, dominate the second act. Wilder depicts the cycle by having two young citizens of Grover's Corners spontaneously disclose their love for each other. Their wedding follows. Symbolically, Wilder causes this single example—the union of Mr. and Mrs. George Gibbs—to represent all of humanity. In this fashion, he celebrates love and the simple verities that pertain to the bonding between man and woman.

In the natural flow of events, Act III presents the idea of death. It opens in a cemetery, but transcends morbidity by emphasizing the beauty of the location, normal rituals of grieving, eternity, and immortality. Each person must die; however, Wilder softens the terror of passage by emphasizing the inner quality of the living that is eternal.

To make his point about the goodness of earth, Wilder utilizes Emily's return to her past as a means of reflecting on homelife from the point of view of the dead. She discovers that the living are beguiled by a false sense of permanence and are too preoccupied with trivialities to savor humble, mundane events.

Overall, Wilder succeeds in re-creating the sublime quality of everyday living. Without moralizing, he imparts to viewers that there is something worthy and noble about their lives. He stresses the simple decency of family relationships. In this way, he dignifies homely details that might otherwise be taken for granted, such as the ironing of a school dress or the stringing of beans for winter meals or the placement of a bouquet on a grave.

In *Our Town*, a fruitful life—even though it receives no extravagant praise from the outside world—bears witness to its own intrinsic worth. It satisfies without fanfare. Ultimately, it concludes—by accident or disease or whatever means death brings it to a close—and transforms itself into a transcendent peace, devoid of recrimination or sadness.

STRUCTURE AND TECHNIQUE

In *Our Town*, Wilder sets himself apart from Eugene O'Neill, Tennessee Williams, William Inge, and other playwrights of the

American theater of his time by his innovations. He uses the typical three-act division as the **basic structure** of his play, but from this point on, he **varies from tradition**. He employs a structure which illuminates a **theme of timelessness** and which allows him to present a generalized view of small-town life in America.

He **structures each act around a central idea**. Act I is called "Daily Life." Interjecting himself as spokesman, the Stage Manager steps out on the stage and narrates simple facts about the town. Then the milkman and paper boy make their rounds. The two families which are the focus of the drama get their children off to school. Later, two of the children return home from school. These short, pictorial scenes are dramatic moments intended to render a **nostalgic picture of everyday activities**. Between the scenes, the Stage Manager interprets for the audience.

Wilder's technique is clearer in the second act where the stage manager explains what is happening in the wedding scene. In his words: "There are a lot of things to be said about a wedding; there are a lot of thoughts that go on during a wedding. . . . We can't get them all into one wedding, naturally, and especially not into a wedding at Grover's Corners." To increase his appeal, Wilder intimates that this is a **universal wedding**. He does so by choosing **predictable aspects** of any American wedding. In similar fashion throughout the play, Wilder presents the **common and recurrent aspects of life**.

The focus of the play then develops from "Daily Life" in the first act to "Love and Marriage" in the second act and to "Death" in the last act. This final act shifts the setting from the streets of Grover's Corners to the cemetery on the hill outside town. Thus, Wilder presents **a unified whole**—human life summed up in three acts, all of which flow along in a perfectly normal pattern.

Wilder reveals a bare stage featuring no scenery and few props. This **minimalist technique**, which he pioneered with *Our Town*, makes everyday objects represent larger structures: a counter becomes the drug store, and a trellis symbolizes a whole house and garden. His purpose in reducing the scope of his staging is to **emphasize ordinary things** and to **restore importance to life's trivia**. By activating the audience's imagination, he stimulates them to conjure up for themselves the larger objects and themes that he is suggesting.

This technique of saying more with less has other purposes. First, by having no definite scenery, the play **transcends** Grover's Corners and **becomes universal**. It can be reproduced on almost any stage in any country. Even in a foreign land, the audience can visualize local towns. Also, Wilder is interested in presenting a true picture of life. To do so, he breaks with realism and demands that members of the audience supply their own up-to-the-minute mental realism to flesh out sets and staging.

LANGUAGE AND STYLE

Wilder was well-grounded in the classics, particularly in the areas of poetry and language. He had great respect for the medium of drama, particularly the use of dialogue as a means of expression. In his homage to theater in an interview conducted by *Paris Review*, Wilder said: "I regard the theater as the greatest of all art forms, the most immediate way in which a human being can share with another the sense of what it is to be a human being. This supremacy of the theater derives from the fact that it is always 'now' on the stage." Even when he employs fantasy, his style reflects a classic sense of restraint, a subtle capturing of dialect, and the rhythms of everyday speech.

Throughout the play, the dialogue reads smoothly and convincingly. For example, as the Stage Manager describes the cemetery, he comments on patriotism: "New Hampshire boys . . . had a notion that the Union ought to be kept together. . . . And they went and died about it." Later, as he looks toward the close of the drama, he comments amiably, "Most everybody's asleep in Grover's Corners." This command of language is the result of a high degree of polish and a recognition of what is appropriate to the level of small town characters.

Wilder's use of poetic imagery is carefully controlled throughout the play to insure a balance with the subject matter. Many of the images derive from nature, especially as it applies to rural life. For instance, Mrs. Webb comments on the location of Emily's blue hair ribbon: "If it were a snake it would bite you." In his evaluation of social aspects of Grover's Corners, Mr. Webb compares the situation to the separation of cream from milk: ". . . I guess we're all hunting like everybody else for a way the diligent and sensible can rise to the top and the lazy and quarrelsome can sink to the bottom."

WILDER'S PHILOSOPHY

Overall, Wilder creates the microcosm of Grover's Corners as a means of expressing an overview of life. Even though the setting remains firmly rooted in small-town affairs, the passage of the 5:45 to Boston and references to New York and Paris tie the story to metropolitan areas. Allusions to the two million inhabitants of Babylon and the location of the town "on the old Pleistocene granite of the Appalachian range" keep the story from bogging down in an isolated locale. Likewise, the education of Joe Crowell, Jr., at Massachusetts Tech and his death on the battlefields in France along with the choice of some residents to be buried in Brooklyn place the story in an ever-widening sphere of interest.

Wilder peoples his microcosm with a surprisingly large and memorable cast of characters. Small references to Miss Foster's marriage "to a fella over in Concord," the Cartwrights' wealth derived from producing blankets at the town's only factory, Principal Wilkins' praise of Emily's school performance, Hank Todd's departure to Maine to become a parson, Uncle Luke's retirement, and the rowdy Saturday night meeting of farmhands at Ellery Greenough's stable form a growing list of citizens, all retaining at least one spark of individuality. Like Mrs. Gibbs filling her apron with feed for her chickens, Wilder parcels out attention to the humblest, least noteworthy residents.

OUR TOWN FROM THE CURRENT PERSPECTIVE

Thornton Wilder's *Our Town* comes in for its share of negative criticism. Most stringent are comments about his refusal to deal with controversial elements of Grover's Corners—particularly, bigotry, alcohol abuse, and sex discrimination. He seems to gloss over the segregation of Polish and Canuck citizens, who appear to reside in a lesser section of town across the tracks, where the Catholic Church is located. Like the three families with Cotahatchee blood, the non-WASP residents of the town seem to blend harmlessly into the landscape—out of sight and out of mind.

In similar fashion, Wilder seems unwilling to tackle the larger question of Simon Stimson's alcoholism and resulting suicide, which receives pointed, but benign acknowledgment from Dr. Ferguson, choir members, Constable Warren, and the undertaker. Even though alcohol consumption was a serious issue at the turn of the century—

when Carry Nation and hatchet-swinging members of the Women's Christian Temperance Union were demolishing saloons and urging drinkers to "take the pledge" – Wilder passes by his opportunity to mount the soapbox. He resorts instead to Dr. Gibbs' tight-lipped comment: "Some people ain't made for small-town life." The playwright even allows Mr. Webb to end the question of local drinking habits with a folksy – and erroneous – truism that "likker" is "right good for snake bite, y'know – always was."

The charge against Wilder of sex discrimination is perhaps overblown. Indeed, while parceling out meaningful work to his male characters, he anchors his female characters within the stifling backwaters of "woman's work," notably schoolteaching, child care, housework, and farm chores. Both Mrs. Webb and Mrs. Gibbs depict marital relationships which are obviously one-sided affairs in which the husband dominates the decision-making process. And Mrs. Gibbs willingly allows her husband to select the destination of family vacations and to browbeat her about her evening at church as though she were a child needing his permission to be out on the town streets after dark.

On the other hand, women were still disenfranchised in 1901 and did not obtain the right to vote until the passage of the Nineteenth Amendment to the Constitution in 1920. Therefore, the acquiescence of Julia Gibbs, Myrtle Webb, and Emily Webb Gibbs to housewifely anonymity seems appropriate to the time and place. It is, by today's standards, unfortunate that George is privileged to make the decision not to go to college while Emily – who is a demonstrably more promising scholar – seems not to have the same choice. Still, young women of Emily's day, particularly those in rural locales, were fortunate just to finish high school.

It is perhaps more significant that Wilder gives no details about Emily's death. Certainly, women died in childbirth at a greater rate in 1913 than now. Such a happening would have seemed commonplace, as does Wally's death from a burst appendix or Mrs. Gibbs' fatal pneumonia. It is odd, however, that the playwright makes no mention of the fate of Emily's infant, especially since he indicates the whereabouts of Emily's four-year-old son on the day of her burial.

Wilder's refuge in these matters seems to be his desire to present a positive – although not completely Pollyanna – portrait of small-town America. To his credit, he nods briefly toward the question of women's rights with Mr. Webb's admission that, as a young groom, he rejected his father's advice to force his wife into obedience. Perhaps even stronger evidence of Wilder's even-handedness is his placement of Emily at the forefront of the play.

It is Wilder's deliberate choice that a woman—obviously well educated, strong-willed, and contemplative—serves as the focus of the drama. Wilder in no way demeans her feelings, desires, and intuitions. Rather, he elevates Emily by allowing her to experience the central transformation. It is through the eyes of a young woman that the audience perceives the key theme.

As Emily experiences the blindness of her own family to the joys of life, she bursts into tears, too overcome by earthly beauty to express herself any other way. Her delicacy and sensitivity are her saving grace. With womanly wisdom, she internalizes the fact that the living are incapable of valuing earthly treasures.

SUGGESTED ESSAY QUESTIONS

(1) Discuss the relationship between the type of hymns that the choir sings—"Art Thou Weary, Art Thou Languid," "Love Divine All Loves Excelling," and "Blest Be the Tie That Binds"—and other aspects of the play.

(2) What descriptive information gives you a vivid portrait of Grover's Corners and surrounding areas?

(3) Why does the Stage Manager assume a role in some of the scenes and not in others? What is the nature of the various roles he plays?

(4) How might this play have evolved without the use of a Stage Manager? Would it have been as effective or memorable?

(5) Why does the playwright stop short of naming what the dead are waiting for?

(6) Why is an omniscient narrator more useful in this type of play than a narrator who is limited in knowledge of the future?

(7) How might George and Emily's relationship have differed if he had gone to college? if she had gone to college?

(8) How does Wilder depict the importance of work to the professionals—law enforcement officer, editor, doctor, teacher—as well as to the farmer, railroad worker, milkman, paper boy, and housewife?

(9) Why do Emily and George, the Gibbses, or the Webbs never use the word *love* when they discuss themselves and their families?

(10) What information might Mrs. Webb have given Emily about marriage? Do you think that George knows any more about married life than Emily?

(11) What minor conflicts cause familial and community friction in Grover's Corners?

(12) Why do Act II and Act III begin with rain? How do the characters respond to the weather?

(13) How would life be different if people could see how it will end for them?

(14) What achievements of civilization does Wilder highlight in the Stage Manager's description of preparations for the cornerstore of the new bank? What are the reasons for each reference?

RELATED RESEARCH PROJECTS

(1) Compare the homespun philosophy of this play to Edgar Lee Masters' *Spoon River Anthology*. Note similar attitudes toward death.

(2) Compare Emily's response to reliving her twelfth birthday with Edna St. Vincent Millay's poem "God's World."

(3) Create a town roll of citizens, giving details about every person mentioned in the play.

(4) Discover why William Jennings Bryan was a popular speaker in his day. Cite homespun philosophy from his speeches that compares with the comments of Mr. Webb and the Stage Manager.

(5) Analyze the lyrics of "Blessed Be the Tie That Binds." Explain why the hymn is appropriate to both weddings and funerals.

(6) Contrast Simon Stimson's fate with that of the title character of Robert Frost's poem "The Death of the Hired Man." Or compare Simon Stimson's life with that of the title characters in two of E. A. Robinson's poems, "Richard Cory" and "Mr. Flood's Party."

SELECTED BIBLIOGRAPHY

BURBANK, REX. *Thornton Wilder*. TWAYNE'S UNITED STATES AUTHORS SERIES. NEW YORK: TWAYNE PUBLISHERS, INC., 1961.

CASTRANOVO, DAVID. *Thornton Wilder*. LITERATURE & LIFE SERIES. NEW YORK: FREDERICK UNGAR PUBLISHING CO.,1986.

COHN, RUBY. *Dialogue in American Drama*. BLOOMINGTON, INDIANA: INDIANA UNIVERSITY PRESS, 1971.

GALLUP, DONALD. *The Journals of Thornton Wilder*. CAMBRIDGE: YALE UNIVERSITY PRESS, 1987.

GREBANIER, BERNARD. *Thornton Wilder*. UNIVERSITY OF MINNESOTA PAMPHLETS ON AMERICAN WRITERS. MINNEAPOLIS: UNIVERSITY OF MINNESOTA PRESS, 1964.

GOLDSTEIN, MALCOLM L. *The Art of Thornton Wilder*. LINCOLN: UNIVERSITY OF NEBRASKA PRESS, 1965.

HARRISON, GILBERT A. *The Enthusiast: A Life of Thornton Wilder*. NEW YORK: TICKNOR & FIELDS, 1983.

KUNER, M.C. *Thornton Wilder: The Bright and the Dark*. TWENTIETH-CENTURY AMERICAN WRITERS SERIES. NEW YORK: THOMAS Y. CROWELL COMPANY, 1972.

Lewis, Allan. *American Plays and Playwrights of the Contemporary Theatre*. Revised Edition. New York: Crown Publishers, Inc., 1970.

Papajewski, Helmut. *Thornton Wilder*. Trans. by John Conway. New York: Frederick Ungar Publishing Co., 1965.

Stresau, Hermann. *Thornton Wilder*. New York: Frederick Ungar Publishing Co., 1971.

NOTES

Cliffs
Math Review
and
Verbal Review
for
Standardized Tests

Use your time efficiently with exactly the review material you need for standardized tests.

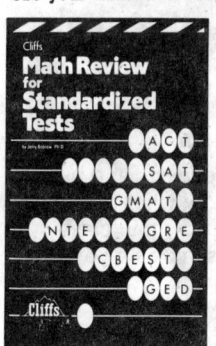

GMAT — SAT — NTE — GRE —
— State Teacher Credential Tests —
PSAT — CBEST — ACT — PPST — GED
and many more!

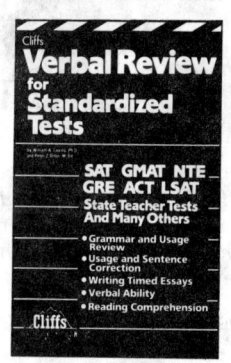

Math Review — 422 pages
- Provides insights and strategies for specific problem types, plus intensive review in the most needed basic skills in arithmetic, algebra, geometry and word problems.
- Includes hundreds of practice problems to reinforce learning at each step in a unique easy-to-use format.

Verbal Review — 375 pages
- Includes a grammar and usage review, dealing specifically with the concepts that exam-makers consistently use in test questions; exercises reinforce concept understanding at each step.
- Extensive practice and strategies in English usage, sentence correction, antonyms, analogies, sentence completion, reading comprehension and timed essay writing.

Cliffs Notes, Inc., P.O. Box 80728, Lincoln, NE 68501

Cliffs Math Review
for Standardized Tests $8.95 _____

Cliffs Verbal Review
for Standardized Tests $7.95 _____

- *Price subject to change without notice*

Cliffs NOTES
P.O. Box 80728
Lincoln, NE 68501

Name _____

Address _____

City _____ State _____ Zip _____

Your Guides to Successful Test Preparation.

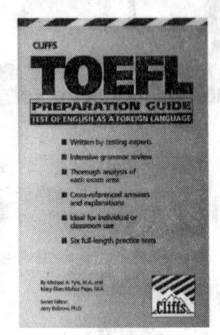

Cliffs Test Preparation Guides
• *Complete* • *Concise* • *Functional* • *In-depth*

Efficient preparation means better test scores. Go with the experts and use *Cliffs Test Preparation Guides*. They focus on helping you know what to expect from each test, and their test-taking techniques have been proven in classroom programs nationwide. Recommended for individual use or as a part of a formal test preparation program.

Publisher's ISBN Prefix 0-8220

Qty.	ISBN	Title	Price	Qty.	ISBN	Title	Price
	2078-5	ACT	8.95		2044-0	Police Sergeant Exam	9.95
	2069-6	CBEST	8.95		2047-5	Police Officer Exam	14.95
	2056-4	CLAST	9.95		2049-1	Police Management Exam	17.95
	2071-8	ELM Review	8.95		2076-9	Praxis I: PPST	9.95
	2077-7	GED	11.95		2017-3	Praxis II: NTE Core Battery	14.95
	2061-0	GMAT	9.95		2074-2	SAT*	9.95
	2073-4	GRE	9.95		2325-3	SAT II*	14.95
	2066-1	LSAT	9.95		2072-6	TASP	8.95
	2046-7	MAT	12.95		2079-3	TOEFL w/cassettes	29.95
	2033-5	Math Review	8.95		2080-7	TOEFL Adv. Prac. (w/cass.)	24.95
	2048-3	MSAT	24.95		2034-3	Verbal Review	7.95
	2020-3	Memory Power for Exams	5.95		2043-2	Writing Proficiency Exam	8.95

Prices subject to change without notice.

Available at your booksellers, or send this form with your check or money order to **Cliffs Notes, Inc.,** P.O. Box 80728, Lincoln, NE 68501 http://www.cliffs.com

☐ Money order ☐ Check payable to Cliffs Notes, Inc.

☐ Visa ☐ Mastercard Signature_____

Card no. _____ Exp. date_____

Signature _____

Name _____

Address _____

City _____ State_____ Zip_____

*GRE, MSAT, Praxis PPST, NTE, TOEFL and Adv. Practice are registered trademarks of ETS. SAT is a registered trademark of CEEB.

Legends In Their Own Time

Ancient civilization is rich with the acts of legendary figures and events. Here are three classic reference books that will help you understand the legends, myths and facts surrounding the dawn of civilization.

Cliffs Notes on Greek Classics and *Cliffs Notes on Roman Classics*— Guides to the idealogy, philosophy and literary influence of ancient civilization.

Cliffs Notes on Mythology—An introduction to the study of various civilizations as they are revealed in myths and legends.

Find these legendary books at your bookstore or order them using the form below.

Yes! I want to add these classics to my library.

Cliffs Notes on Greek Classics   ISBN 0566-2 ($7.95) .... _____

Cliffs Notes on Roman Classics   ISBN 1152-2 ($7.95) .... _____

Cliffs Notes on Mythology   ISBN 0865-3 ($7.95) .... _____

Total $_____

Available at your booksellers, or send this form with your check or money order to **Cliffs Notes, Inc., P.O. Box 80728, Lincoln, NE 68501**
http://www.cliffs.com

☐ Money order ☐ Check payable to Cliffs Notes, Inc.
☐ Visa ☐ Mastercard   Signature_____

Card no. _____ Exp. date _____

Signature _____

Name _____

Address _____

City _____ State _____ Zip_____

get the Cliffs Edge!

Cliffs NOTES, INC.

Think Quick

Now there are more Cliffs Quick Review® titles, providing help with more introductory level courses. Use Quick Reviews to increase your understanding of fundamental principles in a given subject, as well as to prepare for quizzes, midterms and finals.

Do better in the classroom, and on papers and tests with Cliffs Quick Reviews.

Publisher's ISBN Prefix 0-8220

Qty.	ISBN	Title	Price	Total	Qty.	ISBN	Title	Price	Total
	5309-8	Accounting Principles I	9.95			5330-6	Human Nutrition	9.95	
	5302-0	Algebra I	7.95			5331-4	Linear Algebra	9.95	
	5303-9	Algebra II	9.95			5333-0	Microbiology	9.95	
	5300-4	American Government	9.95			5326-8	Organic Chemistry I	9.95	
	5301-2	Anatomy & Physiology	9.95			5335-7	Physical Geology	9.95	
	5304-7	Basic Math & Pre-Algebra	7.95			5337-3	Physics	7.95	
	5306-3	Biology	7.95			5327-6	Psychology	7.95	
	5312-8	Calculus	7.95			5349-7	Statistics	7.95	
	5318-7	Chemistry	7.95			5358-6	Trigonometry	7.95	
	5320-9	Differential Equations	9.95			5360-8	United States History I	7.95	
	5324-1	Economics	7.95			5361-6	United States History II	7.95	
	5329-2	Geometry	7.95			5367-5	Writing Grammar, Usage, & Style	9.95	

Prices subject to change without notice.

Available at your booksellers, or send this form with your check or money order to **Cliffs Notes, Inc., P.O. Box 80728, Lincoln, NE 68501**
http://www.cliffs.com

☐ Money order ☐ Check payable to Cliffs Notes, Inc.

☐ Visa ☐ Mastercard Signature_____

Card no. _____ Exp. date _____

Name _____

Address _____

City _____ State____ Zip____

Telephone (____) _____

Cliffs NOTES

Advanced Placement Demands Advanced Preparation

Cliffs Advanced Placement® study guides are designed to give students that extra edge in doing their best on these important exams. The guides are complete, concise and focused providing you with all the information you need to do your best. Study with Cliffs Advanced Placement study guides for the kind of score that will earn you college credit or advanced standing.

- Thoroughly researched strategies, techniques and information
- Analysis of multiple-choice and essay questions
- Written by testing experts

Item	Qty	Cost Each	Total
AP Biology Preparation Guide		$14.95	$
AP Calculus Preparation Guide		$12.95	$
AP Chemistry Preparation Guide		$12.95	$
AP English Language and Composition Preparation Guide		$10.95	$
AP English Literature and Composition Preparation Guide		$10.95	$
AP U.S. History Preparation Guide		$10.95	$
		TOTAL COST	$

☐ Money Order ☐ Check Made Payable to Cliffs Notes, Inc. ☐ VISA® ☐ MasterCard®

Card Number_____

Expiration Date ____ / ____ / ____ Signature_____

Name _____

Address _____

City_____ State_____ Zip _____

Mail to: CLIFFS NOTES, INC.
P.O. BOX 80728 • LINCOLN, NE 68501

Get the Cliffs Edge!

Cliffs NOTES

Get the Cliffs Edge

Make the most efficient use of your study time. All it takes is an edge--an edge like study guides from Cliffs. Test Preparation Guides and Cliffs Notes are just two of the publications that can help you excel scholastically.

TEST PREPARATION GUIDES

- Enhanced ACT
- AP Biology
- AP Chemistry
- AP English Language and Composition
- AP English Literature and Composition
- AP U.S. History
- CBEST
- CLAST
- ELM Review
- GMAT
- GRE
- LSAT
- MAT
- Math Review for Standardized Tests

- Memory Power
- NTE Core Battery
- Police Officer Examination
- Police Sergeant Examination
- Postal Examinations
- PPST
- SAT I
- TASP™
- TOEFL
- Advanced Practice for the TOEFL
- Verbal Review for Standardized Tests
- WPE
- You Can Pass the GED

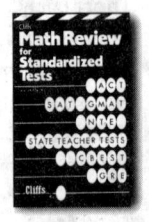

CLIFFS NOTES

More than 200 titles are available. Each provides expert analysis and background of plot, characters and author to make it easier to understand literary masterpieces.

Get the Cliffs Edge!

Cliffs offers a full line of study guides to give you an edge on tests, papers and in classroom discussion. Available wherever books or software are sold or contact: CLIFFS, P.O. Box 80728, Lincoln, NE 68501. Phone: (402) 423-5050.